Living On The Cheap

ISBN 9781520260464

Table of Contents

Living On The Cheap

How to live within your means on a limited income

I first started living as cheaply as I could when my husband was made redundant from his job. We had some money in the bank, but we also had bills that had to be paid, such as the mortgage, telephone, electricity and even a loan. It isn't a nice feeling if you are not in control of your finances and it is always there at the back of your mind, clouding everything you do. Luckily we only had one loan and a couple of mobile 'phone contracts, but I hadn't bargained on the feeling of panic that set in. We had more money going out than we had coming in and if I didn't do something, it would only get worse.

Not knowing when the employment situation would improve, I had to work on a 'worst case scenario', so I cut back on everything. The mobile 'phones went, our fancy TV package was cancelled, along with magazine subscriptions. in fact everything we didn't really need had to go.

I sat down and worked out exactly how much we had coming in and going out. Apart from a terrible shock about how much money we actually spent, I realised that, although we couldn't do much about our income, there was a lot we could do about reducing our outgoings.

After a few weeks, I had it down to a fine art and I had cut my weekly shopping bill down to less than half what it was before. I realised I wasted far too much money. I bought food that we didn't eat, I bought a TV Guide when it was there on the screen of the TV and I bought best quality out of habit when there was no real need. Time for the old pride to step down a notch and start hunting around for bargains.

We all live in a climate of high energy, labour saving devices and electronic gadgets. The days of pie making and cooking a turkey carcass all day to make soup seem like distant memories from our great grandparent's days.

It is totally impractical and unnecessary to go back to those days, but even those of us who work full time can surely spare a few minutes to do the dishes by hand instead of running a half-empty dishwasher. Just for an exercise, work out how much time you spend in front of the TV or playing computer games. If you only do it from 6:30 p.m. until 10:30 p.m. that's 4 hours per night. That's 28 hours per week or three and a half working days, sitting on your backsides being spoon fed entertainment and brainwashed with adverts when you could be washing the dishes, taking the dog for a walk, playing with the children, preparing tomorrow's dinner, or baking a cake. (Microwave cake takes just seven minutes and the recipe is at the end of this book).

We are inundated by begging advertisements that assume we have limitless supplies of money to donate to charities on a monthly basis or purchase frivolous items or food that in most cases we don't really need. Fresh fruit and vegetable shops have all but gone from the high street, but everywhere else you look there are cake shops, hot pie shops and fast food outlets. Supermarkets stock aisles and aisles of pre-packaged food, cakes, biscuits, crisps and pies – easy meals that are high in sugar, fat, salt and additives. Health and beauty products take up acres of space and seem to be full of the fruit and vegetables that are missing from the other shelves!

All this is fine if you want to buy the stuff and live this way, but it's also very expensive for the little you actually get. (Take a second to work out the price of a coffee and a sandwich in a high street café against what it would cost you to make at home). For those of us on a limited fixed income, it's a case of juggling food shopping and constantly worrying about paying those bills.

There are lots of books about household tips, and I don't intend to compete with them. I'm sure there are limitless uses for lemon juice but this isn't that kind of book. This book is about managing on a limited income and squeezing out just a few pennies to put towards a little treat or to save for Christmas. Maybe it could put an extra gallon of fuel in your car or reduce a crippling loan. Whatever your reasons for living frugally, it's entirely up to you how far you take it.

Where To Start

Firstly, take stock of where you are and what you want. If you share your life with others, get them on board. Talk things over with your partner and your children, if they are old enough to understand. You could be changing your lifestyle completely and you must all pull together if this is going to be successful. Living within your means and being debt free will mean a much happier life for all of you if you change just a few thing about your current values and attitudes.

This book is aimed helping you save every last penny you can. You don't have to do anything you don't want to, so please don't think you have do everything in this little book. You can save money by just following any of the suggestions.

However, if you want to **really** save those pennies, get out of debt and finally be in control of your finances, then you must be prepared to put yourself out **a lot.** Your time and effort costs nothing and you could make some real savings to your household budget and get those debts to a manageable level.

The First thing to do is - Get Organised.

Have a look in your fridge and food cupboards and see what is there. Eat up anything that is near its sell-by date. You might have a few strange meals for the next few days but it won't cost you anything. From now on, try not to waste food. It is one of the items in your household budget that is the most expensive, but it is also something that you have control over. You can always freeze left-overs or fry everything up the next day with some mashed potatoes and a bit of grated cheese for 'Bubble & Squeak'.

Most of us have far too much stuff. Have a trawl through your possessions and sell anything you no longer use. Chuck out all those clothes you have been keeping for:

a) - the fashion to come round again, or

b) - until you can squeeze back into them again. If you haven't worn or used anything for four or five years, get it sold. Not only will you have some extra cash, your home will be far less cluttered. The same goes for your children's toys. Advertise in the local paper or put it on an auction site and get some well needed extra cash.

Decide on the things that you can do without.

Is 24/7 free telephone calls or Internet access an absolute necessity, or could you drop down a tariff and use it on evenings and weekends instead? Consider getting rid of the land line altogether and just have a Pay-as-you-go mobile 'phone for emergencies only. You could purchase a low mobile tariff that includes a data package. This means you can use your mobile 'phone as a modem to get on the internet. The cheaper tariffs will have a data limit, but if you absolutely can't do without the internet, this might be for you.

If your children must have a mobile phone for safety concerns, get a pay as you go package and block all numbers but home and immediate family. They will see their friends at school all day. There is no need for them to gossip for hours on a mobile 'phone as well.

If you really have to have a land line package, shop around and find a deal that you can afford. If you have friends and family in far-flung places, learn to write letters again or send them emails rather than using the phone. It's much more exciting to sit down and read a letter that someone has written to you and you can read letters over and over again.

Give up taking sugar or sweeteners in your beverages. Either cut down gradually or go cold turkey and just stop it altogether. You don't need sugar in your drinks and after a couple of weeks you will wonder why you ever used it. Your drinks will taste stronger, you will be healthier and you will save a few pennies. What's stopping you?

Use the car less

Plan your journeys; do less driving and more walking. You'll feel healthier, lose weight and save money.

Newspapers, Books and Magazines

If you can't do without your newspaper or magazines, consider collecting them from the shop instead of having them delivered. Most newsagents will put by magazines for you to collect yourself. Don't forget that libraries carry a selection of daily newspapers that you can read for free in their reading rooms. Not only will you save on the cost of buying a newspaper, but you can utilise the heating in the library instead of having it on at home. All television, satellite or Freeview providers now have their own TV guide built in. You don't really need that TV Guide so don't buy it. More pennies saved.

Fair Weather Friends

Keeping up with the Joneses is fine if you have plenty of money to play that game. Buying stuff you don't need and can't afford to impress someone else or to appease a spoilt child is definitely not going to help your situation. Your children might throw a tantrum, but they'll come round and true friends will be sympathetic and want to help. Anyone who looks down on you because you have less than them does not deserve your friendship or your time. Explain to your friends that you are changing your lifestyle and will be giving up smoking, drinking, clubbing and eating out until you get your finances under control. If they make fun of you or try to talk you out of it, either ask them to join you or find some friends who are more supportive.

Treating the Children

Children are remarkably resilient. If you can't afford the latest must-have new toy or designer clothes for Christmas or Birthday presents, they will have to make do with cheaper or second hand gifts. Look upon any tantrums or sulks as an indicator of how much you have been giving in to emotional blackmail lately. Of course it's understandable to want to shield your children from worry and upset but reaching for the credit card to buy Christmas when you are already in debt will not teach your children how to manage their money. They will just see it as a lesson in how to borrow to get what they want. It won't teach them anything useful, like self-control or moral strength. It's time to be strong for your children.

Also, consider what sort of message you are sending to your children if you slide further into credit card debt, just to buy them toys. They will soon be bored with them anyway or no longer want them as soon as the next new fad comes along. In future, if your little one is upset, try giving them a cuddle and some of your time instead of a sweet or a new toy and see how that goes.

A point though, about peer pressure. If you honestly feel that your child is being picked on or bullied because you cannot afford to buy them the latest fashion fad or toy, you must take steps to address this. Go to their school and explain your situation to the head teacher, or whoever is responsible for the well being of your children and don't give up until something is done about it.

Please, **don't** feel guilty about denying them presents and expensive parties (and believe me, spoilt children will do their level best to make you feel that way). Explain to them that times are hard and you love them very much, but you can't afford to splash out this year. Make it up to them with your **TIME**.

Get some books from the library and read them a story every night. Make up a cheap packed lunch that includes sandwiches or fruit instead of sweets and take them out for a picnic to the local park several times a week. You can take them to the library to choose their own books or go to the second hand shop and buy some jigsaws and board games you can all play as a family. Find out where all the museums, parks and free activities are in your area and take your children along for some family fun.

Believe me, they will remember that far more than designer trainers when they look back on their childhood. If you would rather watch TV and don't want to spend any time with your children, then that's very sad.

Treating Yourself

Cigarettes, Sweets, Take-away Meals and Booze are also very expensive and you will save an absolute fortune if you cut them out.

'But I need a break .... I have to have some luxuries in life....' If I can hear you whining this, **How old are you, six?** Grow up and get a grip!

The reason you have bought this book is because you are either in a financial pickle or you don't have very much money. If you live beyond your means your debts will get bigger and bigger and bigger. Time for you to face facts!

I do understand what it's like. What would you rather have? A delicious take-away, a rented film, a bottle of wine and a box of chocolates because you are short of money and need cheering up? - Or a meal you have cooked yourself for pennies, and watch a film from your collection or that you have recorded from the TV? Most of us spoilt, lazy people would much prefer the former (and I include myself in this).

Well hard luck! You just can't afford it now and you must change your priorities if you want a life where you are in charge of your money. Every time you splurge out on treats for your children or yourself (and cigarettes, booze, sweets and junk food are definitely treats when you are short of money) you will have to cut corners somewhere else or you will be in more debt than you were before. Nobody ever felt guilty by saving money. Trust me – ciggies, sweets and booze are NOT necessities!

Once the wine has been drunk or the chocolates eaten, you will not feel any better than if you had eaten a home cooked plate of egg and chips and a cheap jam tart. You can still have little treats of course, but lower your sights. Don't get that new mobile 'phone or car - keep the old one a bit longer. Don't be tempted to get 'another contract because you will still be paying the same each month'. The idea is to get free from debt, not extend it! Shop around, even for luxuries and try and get the best deals. If you fill in the form at the end of the book with what you spend on shopping, you will probably hand yourself a shock.

If you try and stick within your means, you can treat yourself with what is left over. But if you keep spoiling yourself with needless treats and presents before you pay for necessities... Yes - you will have a quick fix of goodies and then you will be worried about paying those bills and be a little bit more in debt. Was that Take-away or booze really worth it?

Television

Cable or satellite TV is also very expensive and there are now many good free to view channels about. Consider ditching the pay-to-view TV. If you have satellite TV, you can opt out of pay per view but still use the satellite dish for plenty of free channels. You can always find something nice to watch, even if it is on at a strange time.

Record it and watch it at your leisure - that way you can fast forward through all the ad breaks too!

Food

Fancy yourself as a gardener? Even if you only have a window box, you can plant some lettuce and a few spring onions. Buy a grow bag and plant something delicious. If you use a plant food as well, you won't have to throw the grow bag away when you uproot your lovely home grown veg – you can use it again.

If your potatoes go a bit green, don't throw them away, plant them in the garden (or a bucket) somewhere. They won't be as grand as proper seed potatoes, but they will grow.

Buy a garlic, split the cloves and plant them individually, they will all grow as new garlic bulbs. Lettuce, spring onion, cress and radish are really easy to grow from seed. You don't need a huge allotment, you can use old tins if you don't have a garden. You can put some soil in any waterproof container and grow something on your window sill. Have a go and you can eat a simple but tasty, home grown salad whenever you like.

If you get the gardening bug, there are plenty of books, magazines and downloads you can get at a reasonable price. Don't forget second hand, thrift and charity shops. You can also join the library and have a good read for free.

If growing your own vegetables isn't your thing, you can shop at stupid times to take advantage of cheap fresh food that is at the end of its sell-by date. Supermarkets and Grocers will often sell off fresh food much cheaper at opening or closing time or at the end of the week. If you like cakes and pies, try baking your own - there are instructions and recipes further on in this book. If you don't fancy baking but still want cakes and pastries, buy from the cheap end of the market or buy your favourite cake but only eat a little piece each day.

Be creative with cheap food.

If you really don't want to cook, the very least you can do is buy a sack of potatoes. Bread is now very expensive, so instead of having a cheese, ham or bacon sandwich, cook up a portion of potato and fresh, tinned or frozen vegetables. Your sandwich filling is now transformed into a cheap, hot meal. If you live alone, always cook to the fullest capacity, don't bake in a half empty oven. Make enough for two or three meals and freeze the other ones for later.

Take some mashed potato, baked beans and fry up some cheap bacon off cuts or grate some cheese into a bowl of tinned spaghetti and pour over a pile of mashed potato. Lovely!

If you are not working, you have hours of free time to boil up some potatoes or stick of couple of big spuds in the microwave for jacket potato. Instead of buying fish and chips, look out for a packet of cheap salmon offcuts. They sell for just under a pound in all the supermarkets. Put a pile of mashed potato in a microwavable dish and stir in your salmon offcuts and any other veg, like sliced onion, that you have lying around. If you don't want to bother yourself with preparing veg to add to your potato meals, you can make up a cheap vegetable Soup-In-A-Mug (or your favourite flavour), and add that to the potato to give your meal a bit of a zing. Grate some cheap cheese over the top and stick it in the microwave for a delicious fish pie.

Then there's always corn beef hash. It's just chunks of corned beef mashed with cooked potato. Add anything else you have lying around in the way of onions, mushrooms or left over cooked veg, stick it in the oven or microwave with a bit of grated cheese on top and you have another tasty, filling meal.

Make your own microwave chips instead of going to the chip shop and spending a fortune. Scrub your spuds and cut out the eyes. Cut into chips or wedges and arrange on a microwavable pie dish or plate. Brush a bit of oil, butter or margarine over the slices and cook in the microwave for delicious home made fries.

Always look in the Supermarket bargain shelf to find cheap food that is near its sell-by date. Don't forget that bread, butter, cheese, milk and anything you have cooked, freezes well so buy a bargain and freeze it for later.

Put a tin of spaghetti and a tin of minced beef together for instant cheap spaghetti bolognaise and cook in a microwave or in a saucepan on the hob. You can add another can of spaghetti or a can of mashed up tomatoes to bulk it up further and sprinkle in some herbs to add to the flavour. Serve it with a bit of salad or for a tasty treat, make your own garlic bread below.

Don't spend a fortune on garlic bread. You can buy a tube of garlic paste and keep it in the fridge. It is quite expensive, but it lasts a long time and is a fraction of the cost of garlic bread. You can mix half a teaspoon of the paste with any butter, spread or margarine to make your own garlic butter. Spread the garlic butter on any bread you like, add a few dried herbs and toast it under the grill or microwave it.

If you like a sweet, utilise cheap custard powder - the sachets that you just add boiling water to cost pennies. If you add a bit of custard to a bowl of cheap tinned peaches or a slice of cheap cake and a bit of jam, you have an instant cheap pudding, hot or cold.

Heating Water

Always expensive, this. If you have an instant boiler, that's fine - you will only pay for the hot water that actually comes out of the tap. The usual way to heat water is by an immersion tank, which keeps a full tank of water hot all the time, ready for when you might need it- very expensive! If you live alone, or there are just the two of you, consider turning off the immersion heater and boiling a kettle for your hot water needs. If you use a few thrifty tactics, you can cut down your hot water costs.

Washing dishes.

I have a coal-fired range, which means I have lashings of hot water in the winter months, but nothing in the summer, when it isn't being used. I use my electric shower to fill a bucket of hot water for my washing up. It's much cheaper than having the electric immersion heater on all day.

When cooking, rinse off all soiled pots, crockery and utensils with cold water as soon as you are finished with them. Soak everything in cold water and rinse off all soiled food.

When you are ready for the washing up, use the shower or boil as little hot water as you can reasonably get away with and fill a small washing up bowl. Wash the crockery one by one in the little bowl, starting with the cleanest, smallest items first and finishing with the larger pots and pans.

Leave the pots to drain while you use the washing up water to clean down surfaces, microwave and cooker.

Washing Yourself

Have a quick shower rather than taking a bath as it uses much less hot water.

Consider taking a shower on alternate days only, especially in winter.

If you are really worried about your hot water bills, wash at the sink - as many bits as you can reach, which will only use a bowl of hot water, or stand in the bath or shower and try the Sponge Shower below.

Sponge Shower

You will need two clean sponges, a small waterproof table or stool and your little washing up bowl.

Put the waterproof stool in the bath or shower. Fill the bowl with hot water from the kettle and add cold water to a comfortable temperature.

Disrobe and stand in front of the bowl, in the shower or bath.

Squeeze one of the sponges and let it take up some water. Rub on some soap and get it lathered up. Don't put the soapy sponge back in the clean water.

Rub yourself all over with the soapy sponge.

Discard the soapy sponge and take up the clean sponge. Squeeze this sponge in the water and let it take up some clean water.

Hold the sponge over your body and gently squeeze the hot, clean water over your soapy bits to rinse yourself off. Don't hold the sponge over your head like a shower as you won't have enough water for that. Just let it trickle across your shoulders and down the front and back, then gently wipe the soap suds away.

Go from the top to the bottom and take up more clean water as you need it.

Washing Hair

Do as above but hold the clean sponge over your head to rinse off the water. If you are sparing with shampoo and conditioner, you will easily be able to wash your hair with one bowl. And if you let the soapy water and clean water wash over your body, you will get half a body shower as well.

Laundry

If you are lucky enough to have a solid fuel cooker, like an Aga, Rayburn or Wood Burning Stove, then you should always have a couple of kettles on the boil. Load up your washing machine and put the powder or washing tablet in the drawer (see below for my cheap home made washing detergent).

Program the machine for the wash of your choice and get it going, but pour hot water into the soap dispenser drawer from your kettles instead of letting the machine heat it up. You won't stop all of the heating up, but you will save a few pennies of heating time.

Use a very low temperature or cold water only to wash your clothes. Modern washing powders and liquids are very good at washing in extremely low water temperatures. I have experimented and washed clothes in cold water with good results.

Hang the expense and get some plastic washing balls to put in the machine with your washing. These are hard, plastic, ridged balls that roll around with your washing, rubbing it clean so you need much less detergent. You should be able to buy these from reputable companies like Lakeland Plastic in the UK. You will break even after a couple of boxes of detergent and after that you will save money.

While we are on the subject of Washing detergent, do you really need the most expensive one on the shelf? It is just powdered soap and a few chemicals after all. So, unless you are allergic to a particular brand, lower your sights and buy the cheapest washing powder or liquid you can. If you buy from the larger supermarket chains you will see the price per kilogram on shelf under your product, so you can work out which one is the cheapest.

Make Your Own Laundry Detergent

Here is a very simple recipe for making your own washing powder. I use it all the time and it costs less than half the price of name brands. It's powerful stuff so you can use it for cleaning just about anything. Bear in mind though, that it does contain washing soda so it will tarnish some metals if left on it long enough.

You will need:

1 Bar of soap. Use the cheapest soap you can find. There is no need to buy the fancy brand name stuff. You can also use up all your old soap bits.

About 200 ml of washing soda, measured dry.

A whisk of some sort. (I use a balloon whisk but you can use anything you like).

If you want your laundry to smell really nice, you can add a few drops of your favourite essential oil, but if you are going to use fabric softener or you are trying to keep costs down, there is no need.

Grate your bar of soap into a large saucepan and add just enough water to cover it. Heat this on the stove and keep stirring until all the soap has dissolved, then turn off the heat.

In the mean time, pour some boiling water over the washing soda crystals. Use just enough so that they dissolve and pour into the saucepan with the soap. Do not reheat the mixture, just leave it all in the pan to cool.

Whisk away until the mixture foams up and any little lumps have disappeared. You can add a few drops of essential oil at this point if you like.

Return to the pan every now and then and give the mixture another whisk. The mixture should thicken as it cools. When it is completely cold, scoop it into a container. You may find some clean water left at the bottom of the mixture and you can just pour this away.

You can either stick a heaped table spoon into the washing powder dispenser of your machine, or pack the mixture into the plastic lid from an old roll-on deodorant and put the whole thing into the washing machine.

This mixture is safe to use with septic tanks as it has no enzymes or bleach. You will need to wash at a temperature of at least 30 degrees but it will wash laundry well. I keep a stain remover spray handy and use it for stubborn stains or rub a bit of the mixture into really dirty marks.

Try it and see. You will still save money even if you only use it for towels, bedding and every-day laundry and keep your expensive detergent for items that need a lower heat setting or a specialist wash.

Fabric Conditioner

You don't actually need to drench your clothes in fabric softener either, but if you really must, buy from the cheaper end of the scale and don't use as much. A washing machine engineer once told me that we use twice as much powder and fabric conditioner as we need, so lower the temperature you wash at and try cutting the detergent and softener down gradually to see just how little you can use and still get your clothes clean and fresh.

Fold your clothes or hang them up as soon as they are dry and do as little ironing as you can get away with. Hang out your washing to dry instead of using a tumble dryer. If you are working and pushed for time, hang out the big things like towels and bedding and tumble the rest. At least you will save something.

Keeping Yourself Warm

Heating and Electricity are things we can't really do without. Every year the price creeps up and up so it's vital that you do everything you can to shave a few pennies off those bills. Don't leave doors open or lights, radios etc. on when you are not in a room and explain all this to other members of the family.

Even leaving the plugs in your kitchen and bathroom sinks and keeping the toilet lid down can help to save up to £15.00 a year in heating and if you switch off all your appliances instead of leaving them on standby, you can save up to a further £20.00 a year. It doesn't sound much, but it soon mounts up to a noticeable saving to put towards that holiday.

It is vital that you keep yourself warm in cold weather. However, you don't need to whack up the central heating or put the fire on full to keep warm. All that does is heat up your house. If money is tight, there are things you can do to save putting on the heating too much in cold weather.

You can sit inside sleeping bags or wrap up in blankets to help keep warm while sitting in the evenings, reading or watching the television. If you can turn down the heating, even a little, you will save some more pennies. Try not to move about once you are settled for the evening and keep all doors and windows shut. Draw the curtains as soon as it is dusk to keep in any heat and if you don't have draft excluders, make your own by rolling up towels, newspapers or spare blankets and use them anywhere there might be a draught.

Try and keep the whole family together in one room in the evenings, rather than having the lights, televisions, computers and heating on in every room of the house. Keep the bedrooms for sleeping and the living room for watching television and using the computer. Rather than seeing this is a recipe for disaster, see it as an opportunity for some quality family time. If you can all eat around the table and actually talk to each other, it might be fun. You might even play some family games after tea instead of vegetating in front of the TV.

Get yourself settled down with your flask of hot chocolate or the beverage of your choice and make sure anything you might need, like the TV remote, phone or some sandwiches for supper is close at hand.

You can also take your warm sleeping bag to the bedroom, place it in the bed and sleep inside it.

I have heard of families that don't use conventional bedding at all. They all use sleeping bags and pillows on their mattresses instead of sheets and duvets.

One bag to sleep in and one to wash. If you look at it logically, it is more hygienic to wash a sleeping bag every couple of weeks, than to keep a duvet for months or even years without washing or renewing it.

In colder weather you can add blankets and you can always use a throw or duvet cover over the top to make it look nice. All that matters is that you will be nice and warm. Two sleeping bags will also zip together to form a double bag so you and your partner will be nice and cosy with no draughts.

Don't waste money heating empty rooms. If money is really tight, move into one room for the winter. If you can stretch to it, get a bed settee for your living room and put it up at night or, if you live alone, sleep on the settee instead of going to a cold bedroom. Do anything you can to get those winter heating bills down but still keep warm yourself.

Consider getting an electric over-blanket or a spare duvet and put that over you instead of putting the fire on in the evening. It will be much cheaper to use that than having a two-bar electric fire on all night. So, your furniture will be cold! Who cares as long as you are nice and snug under your blanket or in your sleeping bag – TV remote in hand and flask of hot chocolate or coffee at the ready!

Wrap up warmly indoors. So, you might all look a bit daft wearing a woolly hat and a fleece over your day clothes, but you will be warm. If you suffer from the cold or you have poor circulation, wear loose socks and a hat in bed. Use an electric blanket or hot water bottle so that you climb into a warm bed. If you start off warm, you should be able to keep warm through the night if you have enough blankets.

And if you don't have enough blankets, use sheets of newspaper or towels between the blankets and put coats on top of you. Don't let dignity get in the way of a warm night's sleep. And anyway – who is going to see sheets of newspaper between your blankets? Look after yourself and keep warm.

Early to bed, early to rise will also help you to save money. We are designed to sleep better in a cool environment, so turn the heating down or off in the bedrooms. Use an electric blanket or hot water bottles to ensure you climb into a nice, warm bed for the night. It is much, much cheaper to turn off the heating a couple of hours earlier and go to bed at a sensible time, than to sit up until the early hours, watching TV with the fire full on. You can always record a favourite programme to watch the following evening.

You could kill two birds with one stone and put a spare TV in the bedroom. Friends of mine turn off all the heating, take sandwiches, a flask of hot chocolate and the TV remote and climb into bed at seven thirty during the winter months. They have worked out that they can save up to a quarter off their winter heating bill by doing this.

Things to do in Advance

If you know you are soon to be on a small, fixed income, there are a few things you can buy while you are earning that will help you save money in the long term. Here is a list of things that will help. If you are already on a small income – get down those charity shops or have a good look through your cupboards - You may even have some of them!

Thermos flasks for hot water and drinks. Every time you boil a kettle for something, pour any excess hot water into a spare Thermos flask. The next time you need some hot water, you will have some already in your flask to start you off. One or two pennies saved already.

If you are making a hot drink, make twice as much as you need and put the excess in a Thermos. The next time you want a drink, pour yourself one from your flask instead of boiling the kettle again.

A Food Thermos flask.

This is not a special piece of equipment, it is just a Thermos flask with a wide opening so it shouldn't be any dearer than a regular flask. Get one that will take a meal for one person if you are on your own. If there are two people, get one that will take a meal for two, or buy two flasks. A flask operates the same way as a straw box. In other words if you put hot food in, it will keep on cooking.

Try this – First thing in the morning, put everything you need for a stew – meat, stock cubes, potatoes, carrots, onions etc., into a saucepan (make sure the pieces are chopped quite small), and get it boiling for a good ten minutes. Pour the whole lot into the food flask and screw on the lid. Leave it all day and it will work just like a slow cooker. It will be cooked by the evening. It will need heating though and thickening but you have saved a few more pennies.

This works on pasta and rice too so you could make cook a curry in one Thermos and cook the rice in another. Just make sure the flask is as full as possible so there is less air to cool it down and you must make sure that the food is boiled for at least ten minutes to kill any germs. Apart from that, you can be as creative as you like.

Plan your car journeys so that you can get as much done in one trip as possible. That way you will use less fuel. You can transform a simple shopping trip into a fun day out if you use your flasks to make up some hot soup, coffee and sandwiches for a picnic on the journey. There are bound to be parks and free tourist attractions nearby that you haven't visited for years. I lived near a very famous tourist attraction for twenty years and never went there as I was always too busy. As it was on my doorstep, I never really considered it as an outing. Well, now's your chance to see all your free local visitor attractions, museums and parks without any time constrictions.

If you don't like tea from a flask, splash out on one of those cheap portable gas rings that use a little cylinder. The bigger supermarkets sell the cylinders at four or five for a pound. Take tea bags, coffee etc., milk and mugs with you and have a nice hot drink at a fraction of the cost of a café. If you boil the water at home and put it in your Thermos flask it will only take seconds to boil so the gas cannister will last ages.

Carpet Sweeper, Dustpans and Brushes

Elbow grease costs nothing, and by using a sweeper and a dustpan and brush instead of an electric vacuum cleaner, you will not only save money on electricity but you will save the environment and get some exercise as well. If you must use a vacuum cleaner, get one that doesn't need bags, or uses a re-usable dust bag. Paper bags cost a lot of money to replace and every penny saved is worth it.

Batteries

Try to use these as little as possible as they are an expense you can do without. Trawl the second-hand shops for wind-up clocks and watches instead of using battery powered or electric ones. If you can afford it, get some energy saving appliances like wind-up lanterns, torches or battery chargers for your mobile 'phone. Always charge your mobile 'phone in the car if you have one, don't use electricity if you can help it.

Sink Plunger

Don't laugh – apart from saving money on expensive sink cleaning chemicals, you will be helping the environment.

Elbow Grease

When I was growing up, my Mum had a little box under the sink that held the following:

A large bar of hard carbolic soap – this was used for collars and cuffs and they had a good rub with it before going in the washing machine.

A tin of furniture polish and two cloths.

A scrubbing brush.

A box of soap powder for the washing machine.

A bottle of washing up liquid.

A bottle of bleach.

A bottle of disinfectant.

That was it! No fabric softener, no carpet freshener, no plug-in air fresheners, cleaning sprays, paper wipes or fabric refreshers.

Now I'm not suggesting for a moment that we go back in time to that extent, but what's wrong with giving the kitchen table or work surfaces a good, hard rub down with a soft scourer and finishing off with a soapy cloth? People nowadays seem to want to wander around with a scented spray bottle of something different for every conceivable task in every different room, give a little squirt and a half-hearted wipe with a throw-away paper cloth. Why use expensive air fresheners to give your home that 'Just Cleaned' fragrance? Just clean your home for that 'Just Cleaned' fragrance!

Buy or make some cotton washing-up cloths or cut up old cotton tee shirts and sew an old button on one corner. Give your surfaces a good wash down and use the button to loosen any dirt that is stuck to the surface. I keep a good selection and use one a day. I put the used ones in with the towels for a nice clean wash.

If I am not going to wash up the dishes straight away, I put everything in to soak in just plain cold water. Even if something is burned on, a soak overnight will loosen it off without having to use expensive cleaners.

Make your own 'Universal' cleaning spray.

I buy one bottle each of the best quality surface cleaner (floor or surface, it really doesn't matter), a bottle of bleach and a bottle of a pleasantly scented disinfectant. I personally love Zoflora but there are many around to choose from. If you use just one tiny capful of that, you won't need air fresheners and all your surfaces will be extra clean and germ free.

I put one good tablespoon (about one and a half capfuls) of each into a full sized spray bottle and fill the rest up with water. Working on the assumption that we all use way too much of the stuff anyway, this waters it down by eighty (yes eighty) percent.

If you wipe up spills as soon as they occur, there won't be a need for powerful oven cleaners and hob scouring cream. Use your spray bottle and a little bit of elbow grease. I know it's putting yourself out a bit, but you have plenty of time on your hands and it only takes a few seconds. I also keep my old soap ends in a little dish under the sink and push them into stainless steel scourers. Instant soapy scourers!

Charity Shops and Bargain Items

Make use of Bargain Basements and Charity Shops. If you need clothes, bedding, a new purse or handbag or anything at all - try there first.

If you see products when shopping, **that you normally buy,** on special offers, like 'Buy One Get One free', go for it – but only on items you normally buy or you are playing into the supermarket's hands and wasting your precious pennies on stuff you don't need.

Get together with Friends and Family

We all know the old saying 'Two can live as cheaply as one', and it can work to your advantage. Try out your ideas with your friends and maybe share the cooking. You can cook for your friend(s) one day, and they can cook for you the next. You will both save on cooking and heating costs and share some good company. If you have children, they will love to eat with their friends and you can make it sound like a special treat. If you don't have any friends, get some.

If you aren't already, join the local library and any groups that share your interests or take up a new hobby. If you are retired, join a club for senior citizens like the British Legion. Many have subsidised canteens and run outings and special events. You will meet like-minded people and will make new friends. If you are a lone parent, seek out Gingerbread, or other similar clubs. Whatever your circumstances, don't sit at home and mope, join some clubs. Not only will you broaden your outlook, but you will meet lots of new people and have fun. What's more, you will not be at home with the heating on.

The Freezer and Microwave

People don't utilise their freezer nearly enough. In most cases a freezer is full of pre cooked boxes of food, pizzas and pies. Not good for you and far too expensive.

I've seen 'Frozen Grated Cheese' and 'Frozen Chips' at extortionate prices for sale in Supermarket freezer sections. 'Frozen Grated Cheese' for goodness sake! How lazy can these people be? What's wrong with grating your own cheese or buying proper potatoes, washing them and chipping them yourself? You can always do extra and freeze them yourself for free.

Microwaves can do so much more than heat a pizza. If you freeze all your extra meals and leftovers, you can defrost them overnight and heat them up for your very own convenience dinner whenever you like. While the oven is on, it doesn't cost much more to cook twice as much and freeze the extra meal(s). It is much cheaper to re-heat a plated meal in the microwave than to cook it from scratch. I always cook twice as much as I need and freeze the extra meals on a plate. You don't need to have the same meals two days running. Once you have a selection you can mix and match.

If you live alone or there are just the two of you, you can put all the ingredients for a complete stew in any microwave safe container and cook it to perfection in less than half the time and cost of a regular oven. Look out the recipe book that came with your microwave or get a book from the library and learn how to cook wonderful stews, soups and meals all for less time and money. Experiment and see what you can cook in it. More pennies saved!

Take your meal for the next day out of the freezer the night before. Try not to use the defrost facility on your microwave and let the food defrost naturally on its own. More pennies saved!

You don't need to peel potatoes for mashing, ricing or making French fries or chips. Just cut out all the eyes and give the potatoes a good scrub to get off any dirt. We throw away a quarter of our potatoes in edible peelings. So what if your chips have a golden crust and your mashed potato has tasty brown speckles in it... You are saving money on fresh vegetables, (the cost of which has sky-rocketed lately),

Use the cheapest toothpaste and brush your teeth for twice as long.

Put soap ends in an old sock and use as a body scrub or use it to soap down the car.

Unless you have allergies, use soap and shampoo from the cheaper stores and give the fancy, named brand ones a miss. There is no need for fancy shower gels and creams either. It's only perfumed soap for goodness sake!

Use supermarket own bands instead of the more well known branded goods. Chocolate, baked beans and breakfast cereals for example, are all much, much cheaper if you use a less well known brand. Try it and see. There is a difference of taste in some brands of course, and I personally use a favourite ketchup because I like it so much – even if it is one of the more expensive brands. See what you can get away with and get those grocery bills down!

Start buying your cleaning products from the cheaper end of the scale. Try not to fill your shopping trolley with the same things every week out of habit. Look at the price labels and compare. Toilet paper, paper towels, baby wipes etc. can all be bought from bargain shops.

Now might be a good time to move to a cheaper supermarket altogether and shop at the end of the day, when fresh food might be cheaper. If you are a pensioner and your store has a cheaper day for senior citizens, use it.

Start keeping coupons for things that you normally buy and if your favourite supermarket has a loyalty card, use it. Some supermarkets will have special loyalty deals at Christmas or the New Year.

If you must give your Children Easter eggs, buy ordinary chocolate and an Easter Egg Mould to make your own. You can fill them with a little toy or sweeties and wrap them in tin foil for a nice gift. And you will be paying **much** less than a branded boxed version.

Same goes for Christmas selection boxes. Don't buy them – you are paying over the odds for fancy packaging. If you must give a lot of sweets at Christmas, buy chocolate bars individually through the year when they are on special offer. Wrap them in any nice paper you have lying around (start saving pretty bags and wrapping paper now), and play 'Guess the Sweetie' at Christmas. Only 1 small bar per day, no later than the afternoon or the kids will still be hyper at bed time.

Something Else to Think About.

Pensions and Benefits

If you are soon going to be on a UK retirement pension, you can opt to take 25% of that pension in a lump sum, (as at 2006), which could help to pay off any outstanding debts. The weekly amount of your pension will not be as much, but it may be cheaper in the long run to be free of loan and interest payments on any outstanding loans or credit card bills.

If in doubt, ask your Pension provider. If it is going to be a state pension, you can contact the Government well in advance for a pension forecast so you know how much you will be getting.

Go on line and do a Pensions Check. There may be the odd pension from a job you had years ago that is lying there, waiting for you to retire. It might not net you much, but on a low income, even a couple of pounds is a boost.

If you are on a very low income, you may be entitled to extra help with your bills. Go to your local social services to ensure you are getting everything you are entitles to.

Have you considered moving house?

I know it sounds drastic, but if you rattle around in a massive house that is miles from anywhere and costs a fortune to heat and maintain, maybe this is a good time to consider moving to a smaller property in a town or village. You will have easy access to shops, chemists and the doctors. Your heating bills will be considerably smaller, you will be within walking distance of most amenities and you will be near a bus route for trips to the city or to see friends and family.

The Car

Consider downgrading your car to a smaller model that is cheaper to tax and insure and does more miles to the gallon.

If you really love your car, consider using it less. Park somewhere for free instead of paying to park and walk that little bit further to your destination.

Walk the children to school instead of getting the car out for just half a mile. Plan your journeys so that you can get all your shopping and appointments done in one round trip to save fuel.

If you hardly use your vehicle at all, consider selling it and relying on public transport to get around. You can always use the bus, taxi or hire a car for holidays and special occasions. Believe me, the money you save in not having a car will easily pay for any taxi trips you might make.

If you live a fair distance from your local supermarket, consider getting your groceries delivered instead of using the car. Work out the mileage to see if it is cheaper to get you shopping delivered. Depending on the time of day, supermarkets will charge considerably less to deliver, so if you don't have to go out on a certain day, choose a cheap time slot for you delivery and pay less.

Viewed from a certain perspective, a personal vehicle is not a necessity, but a very expensive luxury. If you are going to be on a limited income, now might be time for it to go.

Below is a little chart that shows just how much keeping a car on the road will cost you. Fill it in, with the yearly totals, add them up to make one yearly total and then divide by 52 to give a weekly amount, or 12 to give a monthly amount.

If you don't need to go out on a regular basis, it might be cheaper to ditch the old motor and consider a local transport. Fill in the form below and make up your mind. Remember to add in an amount for buying a new vehicle when your present one needs replacing.

If you do not have to go out every day, it is probably cheaper not to have a car at all and use public transport. If you are retired, you may get a free bus pass from your local council. You may have to limit your travel to certain times of the day, but if you don't have to go to work any more, you can plan your journeys to account for this. Cars cost a lot of money, to buy, to maintain and to run. For the journeys that you must take, for example hospital appointments, you can always use a taxi or a charity bus if your local council runs one. If you put even a fraction of the money that it takes to buy and run a car to one side, you will have plenty money to rent a car for special occasions.

Also, if you do decide to sell your car, you will not only forgo all the expenses associated with it, but you will have a large injection of cash from the sale of it. And don't forget, it isn't written in tablets of stone that you must give up your car forever - if your finances improve you can always buy another one.

Learn to Bake

It isn't as hard as it sounds and really will save you loads of money, especially if you have a sweet tooth and like those cakes and biscuits. Not only will you save loads of cash, you will not be eating harmful or unnecessary additives. It's also fun for the children to join in. Not only will they be spending quality time with you, but they will not be watching the T.V. or up their rooms playing computer games and they will be learning a new skill as well. Good news all round!

I have a rather slapdash approach to cooking although most recipes insist on precise measurements. I think that if you stick to just a few basics, you seem to get a feel for the amounts. Don't get me wrong, I always weigh my ingredients precisely, but one egg is never the same size every time. You will soon get to know if a mixture is too wet or too dry so you can chuck in a bit of flour or add a dash of milk.

I only have one cake recipe and one pastry recipe. All my cakes, pies and puddings are a variation of this. Go on, have a go - it's easy.

All the recipes work at the same temperature as well, so a meat pie or Sunday roast can go in the oven with a fruit cake or a tray of biscuits. If the oven is going to be on anyway, you might as well batch bake and save money by freezing the surplus.

If you are new to baking, there are a few things you will need for my 'One size fits all' recipes. If you have a food processor or mixer, all the better, but if you don't, it doesn't matter. I will assume you are starting from scratch and list the very least you will need in the way of equipment.

Also, for those of you who have never baked before, please note that there are two types of flour. One is called Plain Flour and is used for making pastry. The other is called Self Raising Flour and is used for cakes. If you use the wrong flour, you won't get the result you were hoping for. Always buy the cheapest flour in the supermarket. Flour is flour and you won't be able to taste any difference in these little recipes of mine.

Equipment

Weighing scales (you can get some really cheap ones from the larger supermarkets)

A large bowl, casserole dish or stewing pot for mixing the ingredients.

One or two baking sheets for biscuits and pasties

A loaf tin for cakes or meatloaf.

A muffin tray for muffins and individual puddings

A round tin for pies and flans

A Rolling pin

A cooling rack isn't really essential but it will help to cool biscuits and pasties. You can use the rack from the grill pan if it stands proud on little legs or you can balance it on a couple of books. As long as there is an air flow underneath, your baking will cool properly and not go soggy underneath.

Oven temperature

Commonly called Moderately Hot, this is round about Gas Mark 6, 370 degrees F or 190 degrees C. Pastries, pies and biscuits go on the top shelf of the oven, meat and roasts in the centre and Cakes on the bottom shelf. Simple as that!

If you want to make more cakes, pastry or biscuits than the recipe states you can add more ingredients, but stick to the same proportions. By that I mean you can make double the mixture, but double up on everything in the recipe, not just one or two things.

Basic Cake Mixture

Get your ingredients together before you start. That way you won't be scurrying about the kitchen, madly opening cupboard doors to look for something you may have run out of when you are half way through mixing your stuff and the oven is on.

To make a basic cake you only need 4 ingredients.

For 1 small cake or 6 fairy cakes

3 ounces or 75 grams of sugar

3 ounces or 75 grams of butter, spread or baking margarine

4 ounces or 100 grams of Self Raising Flour

1 egg.

For 1 Large Cake or 10 fairy cakes

4 ounces or 100 grams of sugar

4 ounces or 100 grams of butter, spread or baking margarine

6 ounces of Self Raising Flour

2 eggs

Mix the butter or margarine with the sugar. You can use a fork, spoon, electric whisk or food mixer. It doesn't matter as long as the butter and sugar are well blended together and feel like very stiff cream.

Add the egg and mix that in.

Lastly, add the flour. Blend it well or keep stirring until everything is well mixed.

If you are lucky enough to have a food processor machine, put all the ingredients in at once and wazz away on high speed for a few seconds until everything is mushed.

Now, have a look at your mixture. If it is very hard to move a spoon around and feels heavy, add a some milk, a **teaspoon** at a time, until you get a consistency that will slowly slide off a well heaped tablespoon. Alternatively, if your mixture feels a little sloppy, add some flour, a **teaspoon** at a time until it reaches the correct consistency. You'll soon get to know what feels right.

Load the mixture into whatever tins you have chosen. I use a loaf tin purely because I like an oblong cake. I find it easier to handle if I am decorating it in some way. The finished cake is easier to slice and the resulting slices will fit better into sandwich boxes. I also split the mixture into two loaf tins. It doesn't look much sitting there in the bottom of the tin, but they cook quickly and you can put the two halves together with a filling of your favourite jam or chocolate spread for a fancy cake.

Both the cake and pastry recipes must be put into an oven that is at the right temperature. If you place cake mixture or a pastry dish into a cold oven and then switch it on, it will not cook properly. You must switch on the oven and let it get to the right temperature before you put anything into it. You can switch on your oven before you start to prepare you ingredients and it should be hot by the time you are finished.

Also, if you are batch baking, you want all your items ready to put into the oven at the same time, or the oven will be on all day, waiting while you prepare your next item. If that happens, you have defeated the object of batch baking.

If you want to save pennies and your oven is big enough, prepare all your things before you switch on the oven. Wait until it is the right temperature and put all your things in together.

Now you have a plain sponge under your belt, you can expand you range and make a whole range of lovely cakes using this as a base.

Basic Cake Recipes

Queen of Puddings

You'll need some sliced apples or your favourite jam, mincemeat or some chopped up tinned fruit of your choice. If you are using fresh fruit, cook it up in a little saucepan with some sugar until all the sugar dissolves and the fruit goes soft.

Put a good dollop of jam, syrup, mincemeat or your cooked fruit at the bottom of a baking dish, casserole dish, loaf tin, or a little in the bottom of each muffin or patty tin.

Top up with your cake mixture. Don't overfill your cake tins. Two thirds is enough.

Stick it in the oven on a centre shelf and give it a quick check after 12 minutes. The sponge should be a rich, golden brown colour and look firm. If it wobbles when you jiggle the tin, leave it in the oven for another 5 minutes. When you are pretty sure it is cooked, push a thin bladed knife into the centre and pull it straight up. If the blade comes out clean, the cake is cooked. Keep checking every 5 minutes and when it is done, remove from the oven and wait until everything is cold before you try to get the cake(s) out of the tin.

This is great eaten cold as a cake, or warmed up in the microwave as a hot pudding. Serve on its own, or with squirty cream. We always eat it with that really cheap custard that you get in sachets and just add boiling water. It literally costs pennies and you have a really cheap but delicious pudding.

This mixture will also bake in a microwave oven and can be served hot as a form of sponge pudding or left to cool for cake. I mix the ingredients in a microwave dish to save on washing up. Cook for 7 minutes on a medium setting and test to see if it is cooked. Give it bursts of one minute at a time if it is still not cooked. All microwaves are a little different but you will soon get to know your own.

If you have a dual microwave oven, you can use a microwave and grill proof dish. Cook on medium power and grill combined for 7 minutes and check to see if it is cooked. If the cake still looks undercooked, give it one minute at a time until the top looks golden brown and firm.

Mincemeat Cake

Make up the standard cake mixture but add one ounce (25g) of flour and 2 heaped tablespoons of mincemeat to the bowl. Give it a good stir and bung it in the oven in the cake tin of your choice. It will take a little longer to cook but the resulting cake has a spicy, fruity flavour that can be eaten as a cake, or spread with butter as a sort of malt-loaf.

Madeira Cake

Make up the standard cake mixture and add some orange cake flavouring.

Lemon Sponge

Add some lemon cake flavouring to the standard cake mixture. Cook it in one or two loaf tins. When cold, sandwich the cakes together with lemon curd.

You can add any essence or cake flavouring you like. Even vanilla, added to the basic recipe will add a new dimension to your cake. The flavourings are cheap to buy and you only use a few drops, so your essence will last you a long time. You can also make your own coffee or chocolate essence by dissolving a teaspoon of coffee or hot chocolate powder in a small amount of boiling water. You can also put in chocolate chips or dried mixed fruit for more alternatives. Now you can see how easy it is, you can experiment yourself.

You can slice the cake in half and spread jam, lemon curd or chocolate spread in between to make a fancy sponge.

You can also add mixed fruit, glacé cherries or chocolate chips to the mixture, but this is quite expensive. If you are trying to keep the costs down, stick to cheap jam and lemon curd for a filling.

Pastry

Basic pastry is the easiest thing to make. My pastry only has three ingredients and is the simplest of recipes to work out. The fat is half the weight of the flour. Simple as that!

I always use baking margarine, which is the cheapest fat source for cakes and pastries, but you may use whatever you like. I always use an egg as a mixer, because it's a cheap source of protein and makes a nice, light pastry. Just using water or milk can make pastry hard and brittle. You don't have to use an egg if you really want to keep the cost down - again, the choice is yours.

Basic Pastry Recipe

This will make about 8 jam tarts or top a plated pie.

3 ounces or 75 grams of Baking Margarine, butter or baking spread

6 Ounces or 150 grams of Plain Flour

1 Egg

Put the margarine, butter or spread into a large bowl and add the plain flour. Rub the fat into the flour using your hands, a fork, food processor or mixer, until the mixture resembles breadcrumbs.

Add the egg or an egg sized portion of milk or milk and water mixed, and mix it all together until you get a substance that looks like plasticine (play dough) and is easy to manage. If the mixture is dry, crumbly or bitty, add some milk, a teaspoon at a time until you get the right mixture. If the dough feels wet and sticky, add some flour, a teaspoon at a time, until you get the right feel.

Basic Pastry Recipes

Plated Pie Lid

This is the easiest pastry dish to make and you can put just about anything in it.

Make the standard pastry and lightly scatter some flour over a rolling board or clean table. Flour your hands and rub them over your rolling pin. Roll out the pastry until it is about ¼ of an inch (5mm) thick.

Sweet Pie

Wash and half cook the fruit of your choice. Cook in a microwave or saucepan with a little sugar until the fruit is soft. Don't over cook it or it will turn to mush. For quickness, you can use any tinned fruit you like without cooking it first.

Savoury Pie

Any meat and gravy mixture you like. Left over stew, corned beef, chopped spam and onion, cheese and onion, bacon pieces and tinned tomato. Let you imagination go wild!

1 - Put your ingredients (sweet or savoury), into a shallow dish, flan dish, casserole dish lid or deep plate. Roll out the pastry so that is measures a little bit more than the size of the plate or dish. If the pastry sticks to the rolling pin or the table, scatter more flour but try to use as little as you can get away with.

2 - Place the rolling pin on one edge of the pastry and lift the pastry gently over the rolling pin. Roll the pin so that the pastry slides over the top of the rolling pin. When the pastry is balanced over the top of the rolling pin, you can lift the whole lot carefully and take it to the plate.

3 - Line up the edge of the pastry with the edge of the plate and gently 'unroll' the pastry so that it lies over the plate. You might have to jiggle it about a bit to make sure that all of the plate is covered.

4 - Lift up the plate from underneath with one hand and trim away the excess pastry from the side of the plate with a small knife, turning the plate as you go.

5 - Use a knife to cut a small cross in the centre of the pie to let any steam out.

Pour a bit of milk into a cup and brush the top of the pastry if you want to give it a golden brown colour. If you don't have a pastry brush you can dribble a bit of milk off a teaspoon and spread it around with the back of the spoon.

For the sweet pie, sprinkle a bit of sugar on top of the pastry.

If you want to be creative, you can use any spare bits of pastry to make leaves, or little shapes and glue them on top of the pastry with a bit of milk. Not only does it look nice but it uses up all those extra pieces of pastry.

Put the pie into the hot oven on the top shelf and check after 12 minutes. It the pastry looks pale, leave it for another two minutes. Check every two minutes until the pastry is cooked. It should have a nice, golden brown colour and if you touch it gently with the flat of a knife, it won't stick, but come away clean.

Full Pie

This is constructed just like the plated pie above, but the bottom of the plate, tin or dish is lined with pastry before the ingredients are put in.

Place the filling inside and then put on a pastry lid as for the plated pie above. This uses just over twice as much pastry as the plated pie, so bear that in mind when you are weighing out the ingredients.

Flan

This is an open pie which has the pastry on the bottom only.

Sweet Flan

Roll out the pastry and place on the bottom of a flan case or shallow dish.

Add jam, lemon curd, mincemeat or cooked fruit to just below the top of the pastry

If you have any pastry left after you have made the flan base, roll into long strips and lay over the topping to make a lattice effect.

If you have little pastry cutters and patty tins you can make jam or fruit tarts the same way. Use the cutters to cut little rounds and place in the individual patty hollows. Add the jam or filling. Be careful not to fill more than two thirds of the pastry cases or the jam will boil over and burn.

Bake in a hot oven until the pastry starts to turn brown.

Beware – Jam gets VERY hot so be careful when you take these out of the oven.

Mince Pies are made the same way, but use a smaller cutter to make a little pastry lid to cover the mincemeat. Sprinkle a tiny amount of sugar over the pastry lid to make a crispy topping and serve hot or cold.

Quiche

Roll out the pastry and line the bottom of a flan tin or shallow dish.

Fry some meat (usually bacon) and onions until well cooked and chop into little pieces.

Beat 3 or 4 eggs and half a mug of milk in a jug.

Add the chopped bacon and onions and a bit of chopped tomato if you like

Pour the mixture into the pastry flan.

Bake in a hot oven until the mixture sets.

Eat hot or cold.

Closed Pasties

1 - Roll out the pastry to about ¼ inch (5mm) thick and use a small plate to press out a circle. Place a dollop of filling, sweet or savoury, onto the top half of the circle, leaving ½ inch (13mm) border.

2 - Wet the edges of the pastry with milk and fold the other half of the pastry over to make a half circle pie.

3 - Use the edge of a fork to press the pastry edges together and lift the pasty onto a baking sheet with a fish slice or similar. Brush the pastry with milk to give a nice, golden brown colour if you wish. If you don't have a brush, dribble a bit of milk onto the pastry and spread it around with the back of a teaspoon.

4 - Place into a hot oven on the top shelf for 12 minutes. and then check to see if it is cooked. If the pastry still looks pale, give it another 2 minutes.

Open Pasties

1 - Roll out the pastry to about ¼ inch thick and cut into squares, 4 or 5 inches (100 – 125 mm) in length.

2 - Lay a piece of cooked bacon or thin meat like cooked ham, spam or corned beef on the diagonal.

3 - Sprinkle on some chopped mushroom (fresh or tinned) and a spoonful of chopped tomatoes (fresh or tinned)

4 - Brush the two sides with milk or beaten egg and fold them in like closing a waistcoat.

5 - Use a fish slice or cake slice to lift the pasty onto a baking sheet and sprinkle with grated cheese

6 - Place into a hot oven on the top shelf for 12 minutes. and then check to see if it is cooked. If the pastry still looks pale, give it another 2 minutes. Keep checking until it looks cooked.

You can be creative here and add any filling you like. You can add cooked fruit or jam instead of the savoury filling and sprinkle sugar on the top instead of cheese.

These are also great for a lunch box treat.

Well that's it for the two basic recipes. If you can bake a sponge and make pastry, you have endless variations to enrich your table and palette, as well as saving you loads of money on more expensive, additive filled shop bought items.

Biscuits

Just pastry with extra sugar and fat really, these are cheap to make. Cook in the centre or top of the oven and take them out when they are a nice golden brown. They may be a bit soft when they come out of the oven, but they should crisp up when cold. If they don't, stick them in the oven again for a couple of minutes.

You will need:

3oz or 75 grams of Plain Flour

2oz or 50 grams of butter or margarine

2oz or 50 grams of sugar

The biscuits will taste lovely with just these ingredients, but if you want to be adventurous at this point, you can add any flavouring you like. Any essence works well and you will find them in the cake making shelf in your local supermarket. Vanilla, lemon, orange, strawberry all go down well. You can add mixed fruit or chocolate chips but this will add to the cost.

Either wazz it up in the food processor or stick it all in a bowl and use a fork or your fingers to mix the butter or marg into the flour and sugar until it all combines to make a stiff dough when you add a bit of milk.

You can also take out 1oz of sugar from the mixture and add 2 oz cheese instead for a rich cheesy biscuit.

You should end up with a very stiff, but smooth dough. As before, add a little bit of flour, a teaspoon at a time if the mixture is too wet, or add a teaspoon of milk at a time if the mixture stays like breadcrumbs and will not mix.

Now put a bit of flour on your hands and break off little pieces of dough about walnut size (a third the size of a small egg.)

Place on a baking sheet with plenty of space between them and squash them lightly with your fingers or the back of a fork to flatten them and give a nice decorative touch.

Bake in the centre of the oven until golden brown and lift off with a spatula and cool before eating.

Dog and Cat Treats

These are simple to make and far cheaper than the bought varieties.

You will need:

6 oz plain flour

2 oz butter or margarine

1 of the REALLY cheap stock cubes from your local supermarket.

There is a supermarket chicken stock cube that you can get for pennies and there are many others on the market.

Put the flour in a bowl and rub in the fat.

Dissolve the stock cube in half a cup of boiling water. If it won't dissolve properly, stick it in the microwave for 30 seconds and try again.

Mix it in the flour and fat to get a rolling pastry consistency. If it is a bit dry, add some water. If it is too wet, add a little flour.

Break off small pieces of the pastry and roll into little balls, the right size for your pet and place on a baking sheet.

If you want to be adventurous, (and you have time to spare), you can roll a tiny piece of your pet's regular dry food inside.

Cook along with any pastry dish you have in the oven and take them out when they are golden brown. Don't give any to your pet until they are completely cold. They won't last forever, but they should certainly last as long as the bought varieties and your pet will absolutely love them!

MANAGING YOUR MONEY

It's surprising just how many people are in financial trouble, not because they don't have enough money to live on, but because they don't know how to budget or they cannot live within their means. You must know how much money you have and know what you spend it on if you are going to get control of your money.

In my parent's day, the saying was, "If you can't afford it, don't buy it!" Of course that was before easy credit and our culture of needing instant gratification though purchases. It's very easy to buy a frivolous item on an auction site or go mad with the credit card, particularly for a special occasion, but all those little monthly repayments can add up to a frightening amount.

Also, years ago, we all dealt mainly in cash. My mother budgeted by the simple method of putting her 'bill money' in separate tobacco tins every week... one tin for the electric, one for the rent etc. It was easy to see where the money was going and buying on the 'never never', as it was called then, was kept for small luxuries like Christmas clubs and clothing cheques. A chicken was considered a luxury purchase and a cheque book was used so rarely that it lasted for years.

Most people now have bank accounts, their pay is deposited automatically and bills are paid by direct debit or standing order. It isn't as easy to keep track of your money and there is so much more stuff around to spend it on. Also, handing a credit or debit card over at the checkout doesn't really feel like spending money. If you have a tendency to go mad with the card, get the cash you have budgeted for out of the ATM at the supermarket and use the cash to pay for your shopping. That way you should be more aware of what you are spending and be less likely to go over your budget.

It's also easy to forget that a balance check from the ATM will not take account of the mortgage that comes out tomorrow or a car loan payment in the next few days. Just because it says you have £200.00 plus today, it doesn't mean you can spend that amount unless you know your payment schedule inside out.

The first thing to do is to find out just how much you have and how much you owe.

Worrying about money is not going help the situation, but even if you are not a worrier, burying your head in the sand or telling yourself something will turn up is not going to help either. The best thing to do is to take charge of the situation and try to forestall future problems.

Contact your bank, check your ATM or use your monthly bank statement to get an up to date balance. If you have a credit card, check on the latest statement to see how much you owe. You need a starting point before you work out your finances.

Paying in advance.

Some utility companies offer to take a monthly direct debit to 'help you spread your payments' on quarterly or yearly bills. Good of them to help? **I don't think so**! Not only are you paying these companies in advance, but you are letting them amass huge amounts of interest which should rightly be in your bank. To add insult to injury, some of them charge you for this! Why don't you do it yourself and get that interest?

As I said, if you really do want to save those pennies, you might have to put yourself out quite a bit.

So...Open up a Savings Account for your bill money.

Get one that gives interest on your savings but lets you have fast access to your money. You won't get very much interest on this type of Savings account, but you will get something and you will be far less tempted to dip into it if it is not readily to hand. You can open an account at a bank or post office, or building society, whichever you like.

Even if you just put your bill money away each month and pay the bill when it comes in, you will get a little bit of interest and you won't have to worry when the bill arrives. If you have done your calculations correctly, the money will be sitting in your savings bank ready for you to pay the bill.

Once you have your savings account up and ready, you need to know exactly how much to put in it each month in order to pay your regular bills.

You should now have your starting point from your current bank account and all your credit cards. If you have an overdraft or you are in the red with your bank account, you will need to treat this as a bill that needs to be paid. The same goes for your credit card debt if you have one. In the section further on, we will discuss how you can work out a schedule that will eventually get that debt gone for good.

The thing to do now is to make a list of all your outgoings and incomings.

The most expensive outlay for most homes is heating, cooking and hot water for bathing and laundry. The problem with this huge household bill is that it arrives after you have used your electricity or gas.

It's too late to cut down on your usage once the bill has arrived, but it isn't easy to work out just how much you are using. If you can work out how much you should put by each month towards all your bills, you can bank that amount and forget about the bills until they're due.

Basic Home Economics

It sounds fancy, but it just means working out your incomings and outgoings. Do you know exactly how much you have to spend and how much you have coming in? You will probably be surprised about how much you spend each year. Use the following chart and work it out so you can see for yourself.

Don't cheat by trying to make the figures look better. What's the point of that? You'll only be fooling yourself and it won't work unless you are totally committed.

First, sit yourself down with a cup of tea or coffee and write down how much money you have **coming in** each week or month. Count every penny that comes your way. Wages, pension, alimony, child benefit, interest from savings or shares – everything!

There is a blank form at the back of the book, to help you work out your own finances. Below are two samples of the charts, one for weekly payments and another if you prefer monthly. Use whichever you wish, but don't mix and match them. If you decide on a weekly budget, everything should be weekly based and the same goes for the monthly budget. It looks long-winded, but stick with it. It's the easiest way to work it out and it should look like the example below.

Now for the OUTGOINGS!

The easiest way to work out your monthly or weekly outgoings is work out everything for the year first and then divide it into weekly or monthly parts. It sounds very long winded, but believe me, it is the easiest way. Start with your weekly outgoings, then the monthly ones, quarterly bills and finally the yearly bills like Vehicle tax or yearly subscriptions. It's much easier to add up all your outgoings for the year and then divide them into weekly or monthly chunks, than to take each separate bill and work it out one at a time.

The following charts will help you work out your exact regular outgoings. Fill out each form and write the total at the bottom.

In the **outgoings** weekly section, first put in your **weekly** payments, such as school dinner money, bus fares, grocery shopping, magazines etc. If you like you can start saving your grocery receipts and total them up to give you a good idea what your grocery bill is each week. Don't forget the cigarettes, booze and vehicle expenses such as petrol or diesel – every penny has to be added in or this won't work.

Now, write down how much you have to pay out each **month** in the Monthly section. Firstly, make a list of all the things you have no control of, like rent, telephone, loans, cable TV - anything that has to be paid monthly. If you have credit card debts, or you are in the red at the bank, treat this as a bill that has to paid. If it is a large amount, work out a reasonable monthly amount to pay off the whole loan and write in the monthly amount section as a separate amount to pay each month. From now on, you will be living within your means, and that includes any future credit card purchases. If you live within your means and pay off your outstanding bank overdraft or credit card, you will eventually be debt free. It really is that simple.

Next, make a list of the other bills that you have to pay that are not due on a monthly basis, like quarterly electricity or telephone bills. If you can, get a list of the last four bills for your quarterly charges so you can work out exactly how much you pay for a year. If you can't find all of your quarterly bills, just use one bill and put it in the quarterly chart. If it is a utility bill, remember that Gas or Electricity will be dearer in the winter months because you will probably use more. If you only have a summer bill to go by, add some on.

Sometimes an item will only be paid once a year. Make a list of all the items that must be paid yearly. This will include things such as TV licence, house insurance or Vehicle tax. (There is a form in the Car Section to help you work out your motoring expenses).

Have a look at the following chart if it will help to make the working out easier. There is a blank one at the back of the book for you to fill in yourself. I have only included a few items in each section to give you an idea. When you fill in your blank form you must put in every penny, such as grocery shopping, cigarettes, booze etc.

Now you have all your bills, write down your Income. It's easy to take one from the other to see what is left over for groceries or treats.

Once all the income has been put in the chart, total it all up in the Total Income box.

Now write in the Total weekly or monthly outgoings total from all your workings out. Take one from the other to give your grocery money. If you transfer your weekly or monthly bill amounts into your savings bank you will eventually have enough in there to draw from it every time you have to pay a bill.

This does not mean you can rush out and spend all your grocery money like a greedy child in a sweetie shop. Give it a couple of months and see how you go before you splash out with all the left over cash in case you have forgotten a bill or two.

Even if you find you have money left over, it doesn't mean you can rush out and spend every penny without a worry. There will always be things you haven't accounted for or unforeseen bills. There are things we don't do on a regular basis, like trips to the hairdresser or health charges. A birthday card for a loved one costs the earth nowadays, even if you can't stretch to a gift. You don't have to spend every single penny you have, you can put what is left over in your savings bank for a rainy day, or to save up for a special occasion.

Get yourself a little book if you like, to write down any extra savings you have put by. That way you won't confuse it with your regular bill savings and won't draw out too much when you want to dip in for something.

If there is nothing left once you have worked out your spending, or worse still, you have more going out than you have coming in, decide what you can cut down on or do without. Then do your sums again and see what happens.

If you have a Credit Card loan or Bank overdraft that you can't pay off in full, work out a sensible monthly amount to pay the debt off completely and include that in your monthly bills as a regular payments as if it was a loan to repay. Give yourself a reasonable time scale to repay the loan so that you don't find yourself short.

Use the charts in the way that suits you best. But please don't cheat and put in different figures to make things look better. You are only fooling yourself and it won't work properly if you do that. It's better to allow for more expense and be pleasantly surprised than to mess about with the figures to make it look good on paper and then have nothing left over because you have happily overspent.

Transfer it to your Savings Account

So now you know how much your regular bills are going to be, you can transfer that amount into your savings bank every month. Make sure your bank is one that does not charge you for every transaction. Some of them do, and you don't want to end up with bank charges to pay at the end of the month.

Don't forget though, that if you have a yearly bill, you will need to put into your savings account for a year before the full bill money is there.

If you are starting this budget with no money in reserve, or you have an overdraft, you might not have enough money accumulated in your savings to pay all your bills in full right at the start. If you are worried, use a new Outgoings form to work out just how much extra you will need to put by to pay any bills that are due in the near future. If you have bills that are due soon, they will have to be paid from your existing money, or topped up from your credit card, until you can get yourself straight.

How to Manage your Credit Cards

Used properly, they are a simple way get 30 days free credit and an easy way to pay on line or over the 'phone. They give you protection for anything you buy, should it become lost or damaged at point of sale. They can also be a powerful ally if a company you have bought from goes bust or tries to cheat you. However it's so easy to for credit card debt to spiral away from you.

Some credit cards will actually give you interest on your money if you are in credit with them. If you can find one of them, you have struck gold. Just transfer your monthly amount to your card instead of your savings bank and use it to pay all of your bills when they become due.

If you are on a small income, you won't earn much interest, but you will earn some and you will be in control of your finances instead of worrying about them.

Interest on Credit Cards is Daylight Robbery. Try as hard as you can to pay off all your credit card debts as soon as possible and try to **never** take out cash from your credit card as the interest starts from the day you take the money – not at the end of the month.

Even if you have a massive credit card debt, you can start to get that balance down straight away by paying off a little more that they as for each month. Every journey starts with one little step and it isn't going to fix itself overnight, but make a start today and stick to it.

From now on, pay off **everything** you buy on your card for the current month and try to pay off a little of the outstanding debt as well. At the very least, pay the outstanding interest and a little bit more. If you do that, the loan will shrink much faster than if you just pay the interest they ask for.

It may take a while, but you will eventually be debt free. Switch to a credit card that will take your outstanding balance for an interest free period, which will give you a little time to pay some of it off without adding interest to interest every month.

Get yourself a credit card that gives a cash percentage return on everything you buy and then use it for everything you buy. There are credit cards around that will give you as much as two percent of every penny you spend. Now, two percent doesn't sound much, but if you use your credit card for EVERYTHING you buy, you could net yourself up to £60.00 a year

Some supermarkets have their own credit cards and will give you extra points or bonuses for using their card in store and elsewhere. Take advantage of every loyalty option that comes your way. Some supermarket garages or petrol companies will give you a separate loyalty card to use every time you fill up with fuel. I use one that gives me £5.00 to use in the store every so often.

One thing though, and I can't stress this enough – you must pay your credit card off **IN FULL**, for everything you buy that month from now on or you are just wasting your time and your debt will grow instead of shrink. If you have filled in your expenditure and income forms properly you should now know what you can and cannot afford to spend without going into further debt. If you know you only have £50.00 per week to pay for your groceries, don't spend £51.00. It's as simple as that.

Of course there are bound to be emergencies that crop up from time to time where you will need some extra credit. Your freezer might break down or the car may need some unforeseen repairs. In this case the Credit Card can help ease the burden of a large purchase. Use it by all means, but use it wisely and pay off the debt as soon as you can. Don't use up all your precious money in interest payments for stuff you didn't really need in the first place.

Large Credit Card Debt

Keep your credit card statements and look at them carefully. From now on, add up your regular shopping bills from the statement and pay them in full from your income at the end of the month. If you don't have enough money to pay off your credit card bill for that month in full, have a look now to see where you have overspent and adjust your spending for the next month. You may be new at this and it might take a little time to get into the habit of sticking to your budget but persevere and you will soon get your spending under control. As I said, if you only have £50.00 a week to spend, that is only £7.14 per day, and that isn't very much.

If you have paid a bill by credit card because you didn't have enough time to put the full amount in your savings, pay as much as you can afford in your monthly payment. Add the rest of the bill to your old credit card debt. Now adjust your long term credit card debt by the amount that needs to be cleared in the time scale you have allotted yourself. "Aaaargh!! Complicated!!" I can hear your thoughts. I shall explain.

Say you have a credit card debt of 5000.00 (we will call this the big debt from now on) and you have worked out that you want to pay it off in 5 years. That means you will pay 1000.00 per year, (5000.00 divided by 5), which is 84.00 per month (1000 divided by 12). You should add this amount into your monthly schedule to make sure you can afford to pay it. Don't set yourself an unreasonable goal. If the loan is too much for you to pay it in that time scale, try working it out for eight years, or ten.

When you get your credit card statement, it will show your big debt (probably called outstanding balance or something like that), all your purchases for that month, then the interest and then a minimum amount that you have to pay.

From now on, if your workings out are correct and you have stuck faithfully to your budget, you should have enough in your savings bank to pay for your month's purchases in full, plus the extra 84.00, which will pay off your big debt in 5 years. Now this doesn't allow for interest on the big debt, but you will get that loan down, and as you see it disappear, you will see the interest slowly drop.

Now for the new bill or the unforeseen event. If you find that you cannot pay it off in full from your savings, pay off as much as you can, and add the rest of the balance to your big debt.

For example, you have been paying off your bills for three months then you had to tax the car and the freezer broke down in the same week. Disaster! You have managed to pay off all your monthly shopping bills and you have put aside all your regular bill money in the savings bank, but you can't pay off all the car tax and any of the new freezer bill. You have a shortfall of 463.00. Your old credit card bill of 5000.00 should have had three lots of 84.00 knocked off it so is now standing at 4748.00 in our little world. So add on your shortfall of 463.00 which you couldn't pay off and that puts the big debt up to 5211.00. You still want to be debt free in five years time, so now your monthly total to pay off the big debt in five years is now 86.85 (that's 5211.00 divided by 5 to give 1042.20 per year and then divided by 12 to give 86.85 per month). Put that amount into your weekly schedule to make sure you can afford to pay it and carry on.

Eventually, if you keep on putting your regular bill money aside in your savings bank, you should catch up with yourself and after a few months, there should be enough in your savings account to pay off all your bills in full as they arrive. If you want to get debt free sooner, you can pay more than your allowance for your credit card bill if you can afford it. If not, you can be assured that you are now living within your means, you will be debt free in five years and you won't have to worry about your regular bills ever again.

Remember, this will only work if you pay your month's credit card bill in full plus some money off the big debt. If your big debt is huge, you may not be able to pay it off in 5 years. As long as you pay off everything in full for that month plus a part of the old debt, it must eventually go.

Saving Up

If you want an expensive item, or you know you have a birthday or big function coming up, try saving up for it. If you realised just how much interest you pay on your credit card or on loans, you would see that if you just have a little patience, you can save up and buy your item a lot cheaper. More money for you! Why should you make loan companies rich?

The next time you are tempted to buy something on credit, take a calculator and pad and pen to the store with you. Don't just think about how much the repayments will be, write down how much the monthly repayments are and times it by the amount of months you will be paying back. Add in any costs and loan fees and any deposit you pay and add it all up to find out **exactly** what this item is going to cost you in full.

Also, a note about insurance. Most firms will try to sell you insurance on your purchase. It might not be very much, but ask yourself if you really need it, especially if your home contents are already insured. If insurance is not mentioned by the salesperson, ask them if it is included. You do not have to buy insurance with any purchase you make, so if you don't want it or can't afford it, don't have it.

Now write down the cost of the item if you paid cash for it. See the difference? That's what you will save if you have a little patience and save up for it. If you can afford to pay a loan, you can afford to save up for it in the first place. Have a little patience and self control.

So, from now on, DON'T say to yourself, 'It's only 35.00 per month for the next three years', say to yourself, 'Good Grief! it's 1,260.00 and I can buy it cash for 840.00! That 420.00 difference should be in your bank, not theirs!

You could save 35.00 for just two years and buy it cash. True, it may have gone up in price a little, but you will have the interest on your savings to make up the difference.

Write down on a separate piece of paper, or in a little book, how much you want to save each week or month and transfer it to your savings account. Keep a running total so you know exactly how much you have put by. When you want to dip into your savings, you will be able to see at a glance how much you can take out without breaking unto your bill money.

So instead of worrying yourself sick about paying back a loan for Christmas or a fancy holiday for you and the kids, decide how much you want to pay and save up for it. For instance, if you decide on that you want to spend £150.00 on a summer holiday and it is already October, that leaves you with only nine months before July. Divide £150.00 by 9 and that means you must put 16.67 away each month, or 4.17 a week to make £150.00 by July. Write the weekly or monthly amount of what you want to put by into your schedule and if you can't afford it, LOWER YOUR SIGHTS! Try putting less away for a cheaper holiday, or save a lot less and have your holiday next year instead. If you can't afford it, you can't afford it and that's that. If you are in debt now, it is because you have overspent in the past. Can you honestly remember all those things you had to have at the time, that put you into debt in the first place?

If you really must take out a loan for an emergency item, there is no need to rush off and sign that day. Believe me, these sales people really want your business and they won't want to scare you off. If someone is pressuring you into signing for a loan straight away, there is some catch somewhere. You are probably not buying a kidney dialysis machine for goodness sake - your life is not going to be at risk if you wait one more day!

If you have some savings to spare, try and see if you can buy the item on interest free credit. Usually, interest free items will require a deposit of some kind. Be wary of stores that offer you a luxury item immediately and won't require you to pay for or more two years. If you shop around, you will find that the item is cheaper elsewhere. Not only that, you have saddled yourself with a debt that won't be payable in the near future. Anything could happen in two years time when you have to pay for the item. Have some self control and save up or do without.

If your settee has seen better days, go to a charity furniture store and get one for a fraction of the cost of a new one. Please don't be lured in by the promise of 'buy now, pay later'. Whatever you buy on credit, you will have to pay it back sooner or later. Better to be happy on a cheap, second hand settee, than to be utterly miserable and sick with worry, but sitting in comfort.

NEVER sign for anything there and then in the shop. Always take away any paperwork they give you and say you will think about it. Any reputable shop will be quite happy with this. Look at the paperwork at home where there is no pressure and work out how the extra monthly payment is going to fit into your schedule. Also, think about whether you really, really need this item, and if you do need it, can you get by with a cheaper model.

And don't forget, if you have second thoughts there is always a cooling off period written into any agreement. You don't have to go through with it should you change your mind, even if you have signed on the dotted line.

Debt Problems

If you fill in the forms at the end of the book and find out you have a lot more going out than coming in, or you think that you might be in serious financial difficulty, don't bury your head in the sand. Tell someone – don't bottle it all up as you will only make yourself ill with worry.

If you are in a shared relationship, tell your partner as soon as possible. Hiding it from them will only make you feel worse and a problem shared is a problem halved. Besides that, you can't have your partner thinking everything is fine and spending money like nothing is wrong.

Decide whether you can straighten out the mess on your own by changing your lifestyle or if you need some extra help.

Call or write to your bank and everyone you are in debt with and explain your situation. Offer to pay off the loan in smaller chunks over a longer period.

If you don't feel up to that yourself, get some FREE professional help. First stop in UK would be Citizen's Advice. Their number is in the Phone Book.

There are also local government departments and charities that will offer free help and debt advice for people who need help with their finances.

DON'T be tempted to pay for help from so called 'Debt Management' firms that are springing up all over the internet. They offer a quick fix solution to your problems but many of them will charge a massive 'administration fee' (sometimes hundreds of pounds) for doing the budget that is listed on the back pages, or they will just pass your name to a list of loan companies who specialise in high risk customers. All they will do is offer you another loan at enormous interest rates to 'pay off your existing debts'. Do you really think these companies are interested in you or your problems? Of course not; they are out to make money and will see you as a desperate target so steer clear of them.

If you do find a company that looks good and promises to help, don't sign on the dotted line until you have checked out a few things. There are firms around who state that they are working on government schemes and will sort out all your debt problems. They offer to contact all your creditors and arrange to pay a lesser amount on all your debts. (You can do that yourself for nothing you know!) They will then charge you a fixed sum each month and pay all your creditors for you. It sounds perfect, but before you sign on that dotted line, find out how much of that monthly sum is actually going to pay off those loans and debts and how much the company is keeping for itself. Some firms will keep more than a third of the monthly payment they charge, so although you think you are paying 600.00 per month to clear your debts, only 400.00 is going to the loan companies and the rest is going to the debt management firm in 'Fees' or 'Administration Charges'.

Ask any questions you have before you sign and if you are not sure about anything, go back to Citizen's Advice and get the forms checked out first.

Ask around, phone up your bank, local government office or trawl the internet for some free professional help. Keep looking until you find it – it is out there somewhere. The last thing you want to do at this point is saddle yourself up with more debt, and another week or so isn't going to make that much difference.

Whoever you go to will want a list of your incomings and outgoings, so fill in the blank form at the end of this section and take it along with you so that they can see your expenses and income.

Take along any paperwork for all of your loans and credit cards so that they can see exactly how much you owe.

In some cases it might be necessary to contact all the people to whom you owe money and ask them all to accept less each month until you have settled the debt and got yourself out of financial trouble. You will need all your documentation to get addresses and telephone numbers for all the people you have loans with. Have a look through your paperwork and find out as much information as you can about who to contact.

In many cases, credit cards and banks will have a special phone number for people who are in financial difficulty.

You will find most people are sympathetic and will only be too willing to help. Our local electricity provider has a scheme that will add an existing winter debt onto cheaper summer bills, to help you pay off a debt. It's worth speaking to your Utility provider if you can't pay your bill. They will not want to cut you off – you are a customer after all and it is very bad publicity. They will not be happy with silence on your part though, so don't ignore final demands. There will be a contact number there for people in difficulties so give them a call before you get cut off.

Banks and loan companies will be only too happy to arrange lower payments if it means they will get something on a regular basis.

These people are professionals and they won't look down on you for getting into difficulty. They are there to help you sort yourself out so take the bull by the horns and make that call, or go and see them.

If you think you have a debt problem, don't bottle it all up. Tell someone, your partner, your best friend, your parents, your children, the priest at your local church, or go to an advice centre, but don't feel ashamed and don't think you have to cope all on your own.

However bad you think your situation is, don't ignore it.

It won't go away by itself but please realise, it's only money.

It isn't the end of the world! Just deciding to do something about it will make you feel better and the sooner you start, the sooner you will sort yourself out.

Here are the blank forms to fill in, which will help you sort out your finances. And remember – don't cheat or it won't work and you will only be fooling yourself. If anything, err on the cautious side. Don't add in regular overtime if you don't work it all the time. Play down your incomings and round up your outgoings.

This isn't a test and you have nothing to gain by putting in wrong amounts. If you work on the worst case scenario, all you will have to gain is more money in your pocket at the end of the month.

Get a copy of your bank statement to see what standing orders and direct debits you have and cancel any for things that you don't need any more, like gym memberships. Take it slowly and use the filled in example forms to give you some ideas.

These forms are for you to fill in. They will help you to work out your incomings and outgoings. Please copy them and fill them in. You could use your phone to take a picture and upload it to your imaging software or use a scanner to do the same and blow the images up in size to give you more room.

If you don't want to faff about doing that, just get a pad and write the items down, add them up and write your totals down. As long as you add everything in and write it in the right order, you will get the end result

Blank Forms

Weekly Bills		
Total Weekly Bills		

Monthly Bills		
Total Monthly Bills		

.

Quarterly Bills		
Total Quarterly Bills		

Yearly Bills		
Total Yearly Bills		

Well, that's it. I hope I have helped you to save some money, sort out your finances or be free of debt.

I wish you good luck for the future.

Christine Westhead,

Scotland

About the Author

Christine Westhead was born in Coventry UK
In 1953.

She moved to North East Scotland in 1992 where
Now lives with her husband and an assortment of
pets.

She writes short stories for magazines and is the
author of the Easy Peasy Knitting Machine
Pattern book range

She also writes the 'Starfire' Science Fiction Series

20674751R00051

Printed in Great Britain
by Amazon